D1583590

✳ HISTORY STARTING POINTS ✳

ALEXANDER THE GREAT

and the

ANCIENT GREEKS

DAVID GILL

W

FRANKLIN WATTS
LONDON·SYDNEY

Franklin Watts

First published in Great Britain in 2016
by The Watts Publishing Group

Copyright © The Watts Publishing Group 2016

All rights reserved.

Series editor: Julia Bird
Editor: Sarah Silver
Series designer: Matt Lilly
Picture researcher: Diana Morris

ISBN 978 1 4451 4709 3

Printed in China

Franklin Watts
An imprint of
Hachette Children's Group
Part of The Watts Publishing Group
Carmelite House
50 Victoria Embankment
London EC4Y 0DZ

An Hachette UK Company

www.hachette.co.uk
www.franklinwatts.co.uk

CONTENTS

MEET ALEXANDER THE GREAT

Alexander the Great only lived for 32 years, but he left such a vivid impression that people would remember him for thousands of years.

Philip II of Macedon

Who was Alexander?

Alexander was born into a royal family. His father was King Philip II of Macedon, a kingdom in Macedonia. His mother, Olympias, was Philip II's fourth wife. Alexander became king of Macedon at the age of 20 after his father was murdered.

When did Alexander live?

Alexander was born in 356 BCE. His father had inherited a country where the people were often fighting each other. During his reign, King Philip II managed to bring peace to his kingdom and to Macedonia, and he extended his power over many Greek city-states nearby. Across the Aegean Sea was Philip II's main threat: the powerful Persian **Empire**, ruled by King Darius III.

This marble statue head of Alexander the Great, dates from the first or second century BCE.

4

Ancient Greece, Macedonia and the Persian Empire in the fourth century BCE.

THRACE

ADRIATIC SEA

PELLA

MACEDONIA

PERSIAN EMPIRE

THESSALY

AEGEAN SEA

MOLOSSIA

DELPHI

ATHENS

CORINTH

GREECE

SPARTA

Where did Alexander live?

Alexander was born in the city of Pella in Macedon, part of Macedonia, on the edge of the Greek world. Ancient Greeks living in Athens often looked down on people from Macedonia, seeing them as rough louts with poor manners and very little learning.

Why is Alexander famous?

Alexander is one of the few people in history to be given the title 'Great'. He was given this title because he created a great empire that stretched from Greece all the way to India. On top of this, Alexander is famous for being a military genius who never lost a single battle.

Greek sword

5

ALEXANDER'S LIFE STORY

As a royal prince, Alexander had a great start in life and he made the best of all the privileges he enjoyed. He was fascinated by almost every part of life and his ambition and fearlessness made him one of the greatest rulers of all time.

1 ALEXANDER IS GIVEN AN EXCELLENT EDUCATION. HE LOVES STUDYING POETRY AND MUSIC BUT PREFERS LEARNING ABOUT WAR.

ALEXANDER! PAY ATTENTION.

2

CAVALRY CHARGE!

AT JUST 16 YEARS OF AGE ALEXANDER IS PUT IN CHARGE OF A **CAVALRY** UNIT OF THE ARMY.

3 WHEN ALEXANDER IS 20, HIS FATHER IS MURDERED DURING A THEATRE PERFORMANCE BY ONE OF HIS BODYGUARDS.

4

WOW!

AT PERSEPOLIS, IN PERSIA, ALEXANDER'S ARMY FIND ENOUGH GOLD TO PAY FOR MANY WARS BUT THEY STILL DESTROY THE CITY.

5 ALEXANDER LOVES TO READ THE HEROIC STORIES OF HOW ACHILLES AND ODYSSEUS DEFEATED THE TROJANS.

6

NOTHING IS IMPOSSIBLE!

ALEXANDER AND HIS MEN TRAVEL OVER HUGE MOUNTAINS TO KABUL, AFGHANISTAN AND ON INTO CHINA.

7 ALEXANDER IS A RISK TAKER. HE ALMOST DIES WHEN HE SCALES A WALL IN INDIA WITHOUT HIS MEN.

PAIN IS NOTHING COMPARED TO VICTORY.

8 ALEXANDER RETURNS TO PERSIA VIA THE MAKRAN DESERT. HALF HIS MEN DIE. IT IS A TERRIBLE MISTAKE.

9

ALEXANDER DIES OF A FEVER AT THE AGE OF 32 IN THE ANCIENT CITY OF BABYLON IN IRAQ.

10 MANY FAMOUS PEOPLE, INCLUDING JULIUS CAESAR, VISIT ALEXANDER'S **TOMB** IN EGYPT.

ALEXANDER'S ACHIEVEMENTS WERE GREATER THAN MINE.

GROWING UP

Ancient Greece was made up of a collection of city-states such as Athens and Corinth, each with its own government. Although Alexander grew up in Macedonia on the edge of the Greek world, he was greatly influenced by the Greeks.

Democracy

One of the most powerful Greek city-states was Athens. In 508 BCE a new system of government called **democracy** gave every male citizen of Athens a say in government. They could vote on all decisions that affected Athens. Soon, other city-states adopted democracy too.

Greeks came up with the idea of secret ballots, which simply means a secret vote. They made their choice by placing pebbles into one of two urns or vases.

FASCINATING FACTS

THE WORD 'DEMOCRACY' IS MADE UP OF TWO GREEK WORDS; DEMOS MEANING 'PEOPLE' AND KRATOS WHICH MEANS 'POWER'. SO DEMOCRACY MEANS 'POWER TO THE PEOPLE!'

In the city-states, knowledge was highly prized. Greece became known as a place of learning, where great scholars studied medicine, science, **philosophy**, astronomy, mathematics and drama.

8

Family life

Alexander may have been born into a royal family but it was not a happy home. Alexander often watched his parents argue and fight, for they both had fiery tempers. Alexander's father, King Philip II, was very ambitious. He wanted to bring all the city states of Greece together to launch a massive attack on the Persian Empire. Alexander's mother, Queen Olympias, grew to hate her husband. Many think she had him killed so that her son could be king.

Queen Olympias

This statue of Alexander taming Bucephalus is in Edinburgh, Scotland.

My own research

Bucephalus was a black horse that Alexander rode all through his campaigns. Bucephalus was very dear to Alexander and he was heartbroken when the horse died. Use library books and the Internet to find out how Alexander came to own and tame Bucephalus.

9

EDUCATING ALEXANDER

This bust of Socrates can be seen in the British Museum, London.

Alexander had the best education available. Outdoors, he learnt to ride a horse and hunt wild animals. Indoors, Alexander was taught by the best teachers his father could find, alongside other boys from important families.

Greek philosophers

Ancient Greece was famous for its great thinkers or philosophers. Philosophers, 'lovers of knowledge', constantly question what we know, what we believe and why we believe it. Three of the greatest philosophers in ancient Greece were Socrates, Plato and Aristotle. Aristotle was a pupil of Plato, who was a pupil of Socrates. Who better to teach Alexander than Aristotle?

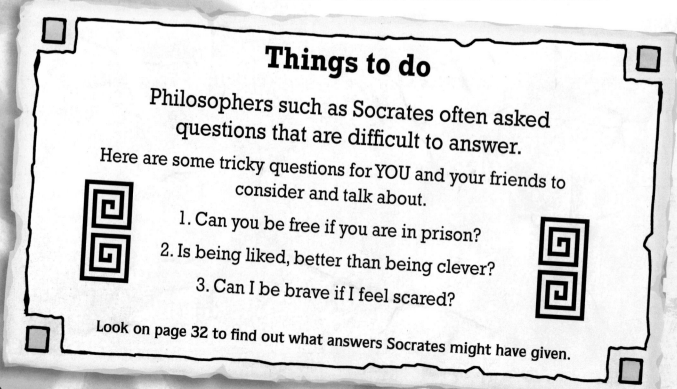

Things to do

Philosophers such as Socrates often asked questions that are difficult to answer.

Here are some tricky questions for YOU and your friends to consider and talk about.

1. Can you be free if you are in prison?

2. Is being liked, better than being clever?

3. Can I be brave if I feel scared?

Look on page 32 to find out what answers Socrates might have given.

10

Aristotle

Alexander's parents hired Aristotle, when Alexander was about 13. We do not know if Alexander enjoyed his lessons with Aristotle but we do know that Alexander believed in spreading Greek ideas throughout the world and Aristotle would certainly have approved of that.

A 19th century engraving of Aristotle teaching Alexander.

Classifying animals

Aristotle had lived on the Greek island of Lesbos where he studied animals very closely. He was the first person to group animals according to their characteristics. For example, are they born live or in eggs? Do they have soft bodies or bodies with a shell?

An ancient Greek plate showing sea animals.

Things to do
Play the classification game

Work in pairs or in two teams. One person or team thinks of an animal. The other has to guess the animal by asking questions where the answer has to be either yes or no, such as:

Can it swim? Does it have two legs?

Has it got a backbone?

Does it lay eggs? Has it got feathers?

11

GREEK MYTHS

Homer, who lived at least 300 years before Alexander, was the great storyteller of ancient Greece. He wrote two of the oldest and greatest stories in history: *The Iliad* and *The Odyssey*.

The Iliad

Achilles is the great hero of *The Iliad*. He journeys to Troy with a Greek army to bring back Helen, Queen of Sparta, who has been snatched away by her lover, Paris, who is a Trojan prince. Homer describes a thrilling duel outside the gates of Troy between Hector, the champion of the Trojans, and Achilles. Guess who wins? In other myths Achilles is killed by Paris, who fires an arrow into his heel, the only part of his body where he could be harmed.

The story of the Trojan horse tells how Odysseus and his men hide inside a giant wooden horse that is pulled inside the city of Troy. At nightfall the Greek soldiers clamber out and open the gates to let the returning Greek army into Troy and overpower its army.

FASCINATING FACTS

PEOPLE CAN SOMETIMES BE SAID TO HAVE AN 'ACHILLES HEEL'. IT MEANS A SMALL WEAKNESS WHICH COULD LEAD TO THEIR DOWNFALL, JUST LIKE ACHILLES.

An engraving showing Achilles with an arrow in his heel.

12

Alexander and Achilles

Alexander loved to read the stories of the hero, Achilles. Alexander went out of his way to visit Troy, where he walked in the footsteps of Achilles, the man he most wanted to be like.

Can you see Medusa's head in this mosaic showing Alexander dressed in his armour?

My own research

Use the Internet or a library to find and read the famous myth of Perseus and Medusa. Why might Alexander have chosen a picture of Medusa's head to put on his chest armour?

The Odyssey

The Odyssey is a collection of stories that Homer probably heard as he was growing up. He stitched them together to create one long poem about Odysseus and his crew as they sailed home from Troy. On his journey Odysseus encountered many dangers including Scylla, a six-headed monster.

GREECE VERSUS PERSIA

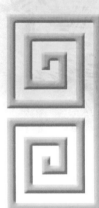

Alexander grew up listening to accounts of battles that had taken place long before he was born between Greek city-states and their old enemy, the Persian Empire. The trouble started when King Darius I of Persia invited the Greek city-states to join his empire, and they refused.

Battle of Marathon, 490 BCE

When the armies of Persia and Greece faced each other on the plain of Marathon, the Greeks were outnumbered two to one. But then the Greek soldiers did something totally unexpected. They ran full speed at the Persians. Their daring act won a stunning victory. The score was Greece 1, Persia 0.

HISTORY LINKS

After the Battle of Marathon, a messenger called Pheidippides ran from Marathon to Athens, a distance of about 42 km, to announce victory over the Persians. When the first modern Olympic Games were held in Athens in 1896 they included a marathon run to commemorate this event.

The men's marathon finish line at the 2012 Olympics in London.

14

Battle of Thermopylae, 480 BCE

At the Battle of Thermopylae an army of 5,000 Greek soldiers held off a huge Persian army for several days. It was a heroic defeat which gave the Athenians enough time to evacuate the people of Athens before the Persians destroyed it. Now the score was Greece 1, Persia 1.

The Persians destroyed the sacred temple on top of the Acropolis. The Parthenon we see today was built after the Persian Wars in the fifth century BCE.

Battle of Salamis, 480 BCE

Xerxes, King of Persia and son of Darius I, knew that if he destroyed the Greek navy, he could control the Mediterranean Sea. But Xerxes was tricked into sending his ships into a trap. Warships from Greek city-states surrounded the Persian ships and smashed their wooden **hulls**. Only half of the Persian fleet made it home. The score was Greece 2, Persia 1. Greece now had the most powerful navy in the Mediterranean Sea.

My own research

Persia is now known as Iran. Use an atlas to find Iran. What are the five biggest countries bordering it?

An artist's impression of the Battle of Salamis.

15

ALEXANDER'S ARMY

Alexander was lucky to inherit a well-trained army from his father, King Philip II. When Philip suddenly died, Alexander simply did what his father was planning to do, and took on the Persian army.

Greek hoplite

A Greek hoplite soldier was protected by a round shield called a hoplon, made from wood with a bronze face. He wore a bronze helmet and armour on his chest, waist and shins. A hoplite had a short sword, about 60 cm long, and a spear 2 m to 3 m in length.

Ancient pottery showing Greek soldiers

Things to do

FOLD

Use this diagram to create your own Greek helmet.

Fold an A3 sheet of paper in half and draw this shape onto one side. Cut out the design and unfold the paper. Cut a strip of paper or card to go around the back of your head. Adjust the strip to fit your head, and then tape it to the helmet.

16

Ideas for battle

Alexander's father developed the idea of having rows of soldiers form a **phalanx**, each armed with a long spear called a sarissa. At around 5 m in length, the sarissa made it very difficult for an enemy to get close.

My own research

The Battle of Gaugamela was the most important battle Alexander ever fought. Use library books or the Internet to find out who he was fighting, where it took place and what happened.

A sarissa

A phalanx of soldiers, each holding a sarissa.

Alexander: a brilliant general

Alexander was fascinated by how wars were fought and he could guess the battle tactics of his enemies better than anyone. At the Battle of Granicus, Alexander saw how King

Darius III had positioned his army in a defensive formation. He interpreted this as a sign of weakness and immediately led a head-on attack. The Persian army crumbled.

17

GREEK BELIEFS

People in ancient Greece believed that gods and goddesses affected every part of their lives: from whether their crops grew well, to whether they lived or died. Alexander was careful to keep the gods and goddesses on his side.

Greek gods and goddesses

The Greeks worshipped many gods. These are some of the main ones:

Zeus

King of the gods

Poseidon

God of the sea

Hypnos

God of sleep

Hades

God of the underworld and the dead

Aphrodite

Goddess of love and beauty

Apollo

God of music, poetry and the sun

FASCINATING FACTS

THE AMERICAN SPACE AGENCY (NASA) CHOSE THE NAME 'APOLLO' FOR THEIR SPACE PROGRAMME IN THE 1960s AFTER ONE OF ITS DIRECTORS SAW AN IMAGE OF APOLLO RIDING HIS CHARIOT ACROSS THE SUN.

Pleasing the gods

The Greeks worshipped gods and goddesses in temples and at **shrines**. Shrines could be big or small, on the street corner or in a person's home. People had favourite gods or godesses, who they hoped would look after them. Alexander's personal god was Dionysus, god of wine-making. To keep the gods happy people made sacrifices or brought gifts to them. Alexander's mother, Olympias, sometimes danced wildly before a shrine of Dionysus in order to gain his favour.

Greek women dancing

The most famous oracle in all of Greece was at the Temple of Apollo at Delphi, 180 km northwest of Athens.

Seeking signs

The Greeks turned to their gods when making important decisions. Sometimes that meant visiting an **oracle**. When Alexander was in Egypt he travelled 240 km across the desert to ask an oracle about the future war with Persia. The oracle told him he was the son of a god and he would see victory. Imagine what that did to the confidence of his soldiers!

19

ALEXANDER'S EPIC JOURNEY

Alexander left Greece in 334 BCE with an army of about 35,000 men. His aim was to defeat King Darius III and his Persian army. Alexander did not know it then but he would never again set foot on Greek soil.

A physical challenge

For over 11 years Alexander was constantly on the move, fighting endless battles, creating new cities and overcoming terrible hardships on the way. He and his army travelled over the dry, Makran desert (below), crossed dangerous rivers and climbed the Hindu Kush mountains (above). On the way back from India over half of Alexander's men died because there was no water in the barren desert they were travelling through.

Alexander and his army suffered freezing temperatures in the mountains and overpowering heat in the deserts.

Things to do

On his epic journey Alexander travelled more than 32,000 km through 16 countries. Use this map and an atlas to un-jumble the names of eight modern-day countries he travelled through.

1. ARIN 2. RAIQ 3. NAKITASP 4. NAICH 5. YURKET 6. PEGTY 7. RAISY 8. DIANI

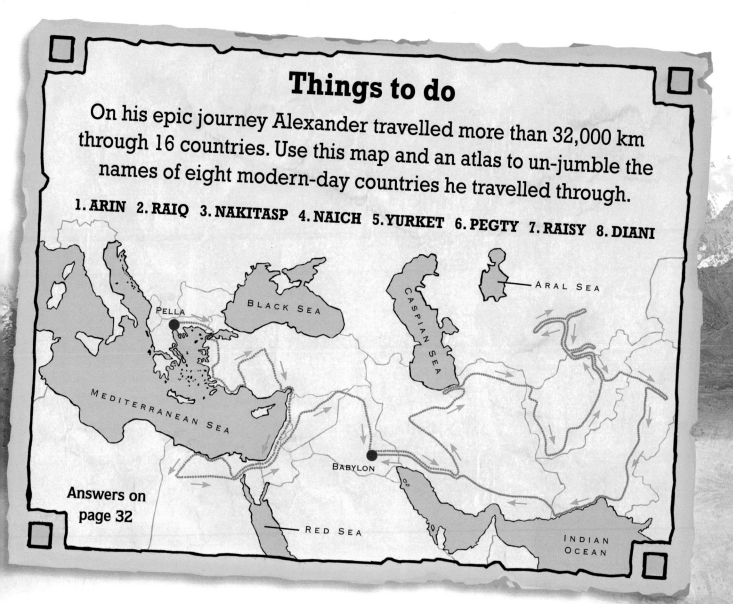

ARAL SEA

CASPIAN SEA

BLACK SEA

PELLA

MEDITERRANEAN SEA

BABYLON

Answers on page 32

RED SEA

INDIAN OCEAN

A mental challenge

Alexander had to keep up the spirits of his soldiers for 11 years. This was made easier by winning every battle. But during 'down times' when there was nothing much to do, Alexander organised games. The men took part in horse-racing, wrestling and other sporting competitions. We know that Alexander and his men passed the time playing dice using the same kind of six-sided dice we have today.

Ancient Greek pottery showing people playing a dice game

21

ALEXANDER IN EGYPT

The Greeks admired the ancient civilisation of Egypt. They knew all about the great pyramids and its grand temples. Alexander knew his fame would soar to new heights if he were made king, or **pharaoh**, of Egypt.

A Greek pharaoh

When Alexander reached Egypt he was welcomed with open arms. Egyptians hated the Persians because they did not respect their gods. Alexander, on the other hand, gave money to the temples and gifts to Egyptian gods. Alexander **conquered** Egypt without raising a single sword. He was made pharaoh in 332 BCE, and kept this title until his death.

Alexandria: a city is born

The port of Alexandria in Egypt is named after Alexander who realised the importance of building a brand new city at the mouth of the River Nile. It would become the busiest port in the world and it would be the site of the Pharos Lighthouse, the tallest lighthouse anyone had ever seen and one of the **Seven Wonders of the World**.

An artist's impression of the Pharos Lighthouse

22

HISTORY LINKS

ALEXANDER PLANNED THE CITY OF ALEXANDRIA HIMSELF. HE MARKED OUT THE STREETS USING FLOUR. ITS DESIGN WAS VERY SIMILAR TO MODERN CITIES IN THE USA SUCH AS NEW YORK, AS BOTH ARE BUILT ON A SIMPLE GRID SYSTEM.

Alexandria and New York both have straight roads and buildings built in a grid pattern.

The great city of learning

Alexander had a dream of attracting the best brains of the ancient world to Alexandria where they would be free to think, teach and develop new ideas. When he died his good friend Ptolemy became pharaoh, and he saw Alexander's dream come to life. Ptolemy built the fabulous Library of Alexandria and many discoveries were made by people living in Alexandria. Archimedes invented a machine to draw water from a river. Much later, Heron of Alexandria invented the first vending machine. It was used to give out holy water to visitors who inserted a coin into a slot.

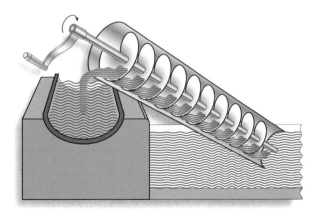

An Archimedes Screw is named after its Greek inventor, Archimedes.

ALEXANDER IN INDIA

Alexander pursued a Persian leader called Bessus all the way to Afghanistan. After his capture, Alexander continued east towards India.

REPORT FROM THE TIMES

326 BCE

VICTORY FOR ALEXANDER AT BATTLE OF HYDASPES

THIS NEWSPAPER CALLS ON ALL GREEKS TO SACRIFICE TO THE GODS IN CELEBRATION OF ALEXANDER'S ANNIHILATION OF THE INDIAN ARMY.

Five days ago we reported that the two armies had camped on opposite banks of the Hydaspes river. Messengers from India now tell us that Alexander tricked King Porus and made a surprise attack. Despite their army having 200 war elephants our brave hoplites and cavalry won the day. Special praise goes to the Iranian archers who showed enormous skill firing their deadly arrows whilst galloping full speed on horseback.

A coin showing Alexander attacking Porus

A GREAT AND GLORIOUS TRIUMPH!

FASCINATING FACTS

As Greek soldiers travelled on their epic journey many asked foreign women to join them. When the army returned to Susa in Persia, Alexander held a huge wedding ceremony where 10,000 men, including Alexander, got married all at the same time.

An artist's impression of the wedding at Susa

24

Staying afloat

In India, Alexander had to cross several large rivers that were swollen by melting snow from the mountains nearby. Alexander's men carried collapsible boats over land. On the water the boats were kept afloat by enormous leather bags filled with straw.

How does a boat float?

Archimedes, who studied in Alexandria, is famous for leaping out of his bath and running naked down the street shouting EUREKA! He had suddenly realised an important principle about floating and sinking. When a boat is put in water it **displaces** some of the water. If the weight of the boat that is under the water is lighter than the water it has displaced then it will float. If not, it won't.

Archimedes realised that water was being displaced when he was in the bath.

The keel on a boat displaces the water and makes it float.

KEEL

25

HOW DO WE KNOW?

Even during his short life people realised Alexander was special. His many achievements were remarkable for such a young man and so people wrote about him while he was alive and after his death.

Sources to learn from

In places Alexander visited, many stories have been handed down through families, across time, about his deeds, good and bad. He is still remembered today in Egypt, Iran, Iraq and Afghanistan though he died nearly 2,500 years ago.

Although there are many written accounts of Alexander's life and achievements, none survive that were written during his lifetime. The writer Plutarch wrote a biography of Alexander about 350 years after his death and the writer Arrian wrote a history of Alexander about 450 years after his death.

An illustration from an 18th century Persian manuscript, which tells the story of Alexander the Great.

We can learn about Alexander and where he went from the many cities he created. The cities of Kandahar and Herat in Afghanistan were both founded by Alexander.

Today Herat is the third largest city in Afghanistan.

The Great or the Terrible?

In parts of the world Alexander is still remembered as a kind of devil, but if you ask a military leader he may say Alexander was the greatest general of all time. Could Alexander have been both great and terrible?

Give Alexander a score from 0 to 10 for each of these facts about him.

Terrible		Bad			Reasonable		Good			Great
0	1	2	3	4	5	6	7	8	9	10

• In the city of Tyre, Alexander crucified over 2,000 people who refused to surrender.

• In the desert Alexander was offered water but he poured it away saying, that if his men could not drink, neither would he.

• Alexander was 18 years old when he led his troops to a stunning victory against the army of Athens.

• Alexander was so impressed with the way his enemy, King Porus, had led the Indian army at the Batttle of Hydaspes that he allowed him to remain as king and ruler.

• When Alexander's men said they wanted to go home, Alexander refused to see anyone for two days.

• At a party Alexander stabbed to death an old, loyal soldier because he had dared to criticise him.

• During ten years of war, Alexander never lost a battle.

• Alexander told his men he wanted to be worshipped as a god.

Now add up the scores and divide the total by eight to see where Alexander fits on this scale.

27

ALEXANDER'S LEGACY

Over the years many great leaders have studied Alexander's life, especially the battles he fought. Most were envious of his achievements. He was a leader whom others measured themselves by.

Spread of Greek culture

As Alexander conquered one country after another on his way east to India, he took with him traditional Greek customs and ideas. Some of these had a lasting effect on the people living in those countries. For centuries, in places like India and Afghanistan it was common to see a Buddhist dressed in Greek costume.

This statue of a Buddha is from Pakistan. It dates back to the first or second century CE.

FASCINATING FACTS

THE NEW TESTAMENT PART OF THE BIBLE, WHICH TELLS THE STORY OF JESUS, WAS WRITTEN IN THE GREEK LANGUAGE SIMPLY BECAUSE ALEXANDER HAD CONQUERED ISRAEL, THE PLACE OF JESUS' BIRTH.

Cities

Wherever he went in the world Alexander wanted to create new cities, all named after him. The Greek historian Plutarch recorded at least 70 cities founded by Alexander, but we cannot be sure of the exact number. Most are no longer called Alexandria, with one important exception. Alexandria is the second biggest city in Egypt and is still one of the most important ports on the Mediterranean Sea.

The city of Alexandria was founded by Alexander the Great in 331 BCE.

A carved relief showing Alexander the Great in battle

Military genius

Alexander fought as many as 17 battles and besieged numerous places to create the largest empire anyone had ever known. He won every battle he fought, which makes him very special amongst the great generals of the past. Army officers today still study Alexander's tactics to find out how he won all those battles.

A strong personality

Perhaps the most lasting effect on history is not Alexander's many achievements but the power of his personality. Those who have studied his life often find that what impresses them most is Alexander, the man. Though he thought of himself as a god, he fought and suffered alongside his men. While he could be arrogant and cruel he was also generous and kind. His army worshipped him. Why else would they have followed him to the ends of the Earth?

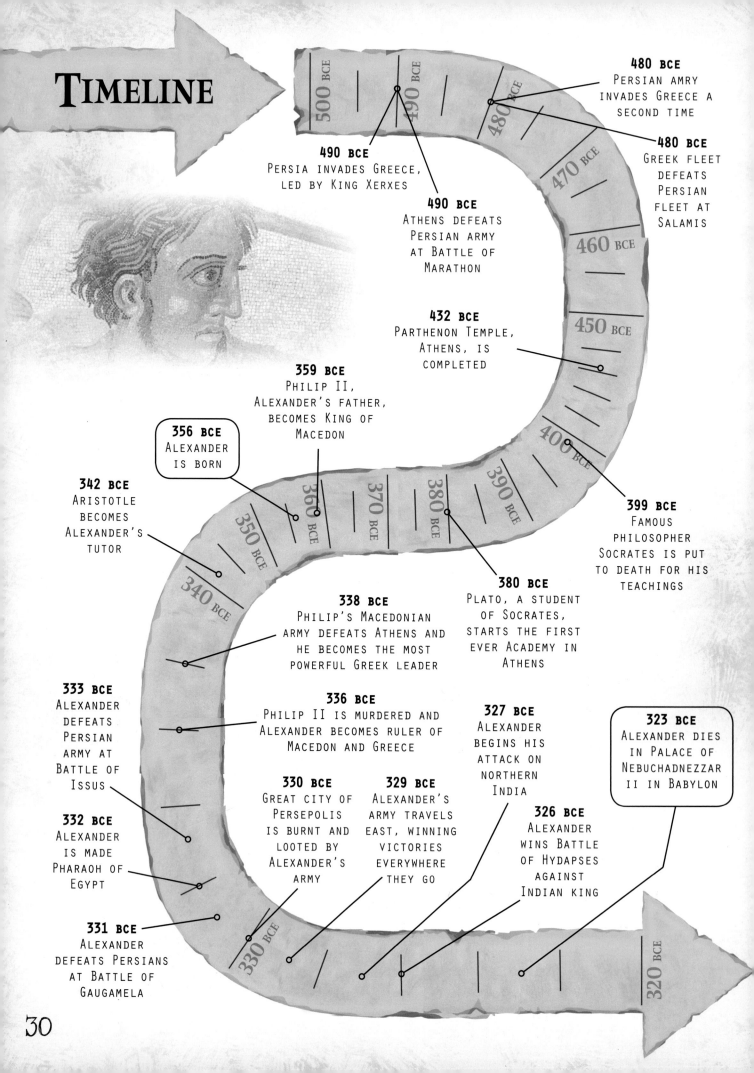

TIMELINE

490 BCE
PERSIA INVADES GREECE, LED BY KING XERXES

490 BCE
ATHENS DEFEATS PERSIAN ARMY AT BATTLE OF MARATHON

480 BCE
PERSIAN AMRY INVADES GREECE A SECOND TIME

480 BCE
GREEK FLEET DEFEATS PERSIAN FLEET AT SALAMIS

432 BCE
PARTHENON TEMPLE, ATHENS, IS COMPLETED

399 BCE
FAMOUS PHILOSOPHER SOCRATES IS PUT TO DEATH FOR HIS TEACHINGS

380 BCE
PLATO, A STUDENT OF SOCRATES, STARTS THE FIRST EVER ACADEMY IN ATHENS

359 BCE
PHILIP II, ALEXANDER'S FATHER, BECOMES KING OF MACEDON

356 BCE
ALEXANDER IS BORN

342 BCE
ARISTOTLE BECOMES ALEXANDER'S TUTOR

338 BCE
PHILIP'S MACEDONIAN ARMY DEFEATS ATHENS AND HE BECOMES THE MOST POWERFUL GREEK LEADER

336 BCE
PHILIP II IS MURDERED AND ALEXANDER BECOMES RULER OF MACEDON AND GREECE

333 BCE
ALEXANDER DEFEATS PERSIAN ARMY AT BATTLE OF ISSUS

332 BCE
ALEXANDER IS MADE PHARAOH OF EGYPT

331 BCE
ALEXANDER DEFEATS PERSIANS AT BATTLE OF GAUGAMELA

330 BCE
GREAT CITY OF PERSEPOLIS IS BURNT AND LOOTED BY ALEXANDER'S ARMY

329 BCE
ALEXANDER'S ARMY TRAVELS EAST, WINNING VICTORIES EVERYWHERE THEY GO

327 BCE
ALEXANDER BEGINS HIS ATTACK ON NORTHERN INDIA

326 BCE
ALEXANDER WINS BATTLE OF HYDASPES AGAINST INDIAN KING

323 BCE
ALEXANDER DIES IN PALACE OF NEBUCHADNEZZAR II IN BABYLON

GLOSSARY

Cavalry the part of the army that fought on horses

Conquer to take over a place, usually by force

Democracy a system of government in which people vote to elect their representatives

Displace to move something from its original position

Empire a group of countries or states controlled by one ruler

Hull the bottom part of a ship, that goes in the water

Oracle in ancient Greece, a priest or priestess who passed on messages from the gods

Phalanx a group of people or things standing very close together

Pharaoh a ruler of ancient Egypt

Philosophy the study of knowledge and truth in human life

Seven Wonders of the World the seven most spectacular manmade structures of ancient times

Shrine a place where people come to worship because it is connected with a holy person or event

Tomb a large grave, especially one built of stone, above or below the ground

THE GREAT ALEXANDER THE GREAT QUIZ

1. Who was Alexander's hero?
2. What was the name of Alexander's famous teacher?
3. Which Greek god was King of the gods?
4. How did Alexander's father die?
5. What are the names of three cities founded by Alexander?

6. In what year did the modern Olympics begin?
7. What was the name of Alexander's precious horse?
8. Which empire was Alexander's greatest enemy?
9. What is a hoplite?
10. Where did Alexander find enough gold to pay for his wars?

Answers on page 32

Achilles 7, 12–13
Afghanistan 7, 20, 24, 26, 28
Alexander
　education 6, 10–11
　family 4, 9
　military leader 5, 16–29
　pharaoh 22–23
Alexandria 22–23, 25, 29
Apollo 18–19
Archimedes 23, 25
Aristotle 10–11
army 6, 14–17, 20–29
Athens 5, 8, 14–15, 19, 27

Babylon 7, 21, 26, 27
Bechephalus 9
beliefs 18–19
Buddhists 28

Caesar, Julius 7
city-states 4, 8–9, 14–15

democracy 8
Egypt 7, 19, 21, 22–23, 26, 29
gods/goddesses 18–19, 22, 24, 27, 29

government 8

Heron of Alexandria 23
Homer 12–13
hoplites 14–17, 24, 27

India 5, 7, 20, 21, 24–25, 27, 28

King Darius I 14–15
King Darius III 4, 17, 20
King Philip II 4, 6, 9, 10, 16, 17
King Porus 24, 27
King Xerxes 15

Library of Alexandria 23

Macedonia 4–5, 8
Makran 7, 20
marathons 14
Medusa 13
myths 12–13

NASA 18
Odysseus 7, 12, 13
Olympic Games 14, 19
oracles 19

Pella 5, 21

Persepolis 6
Perseus 13
Persian Empire 4–5, 9, 14–17, 20–22, 24
phalanx 17
Pharos Lighthouse 22
philosophy/philosophers 8, 10–11
Plato 10
Plutarch 26, 29
Ptolemy 23

Queen Olympias 4, 9, 19

religion 18–19

Socrates 10
soldiers 14–17, 21, 24, 27, 29
Susa 24

temples 15, 19, 22
The Iliad 12–13
The Odyssey 12, 13
Troy/Trojans 7, 12, 13

warships 15
weapons 16–17

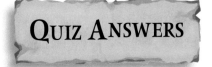
QUIZ ANSWERS

Things to do, page 10: 1. Yes, because your mind is free to think and to imagine. **2.** It is better to be clever because people's views about you can change but no one can take away your knowledge and ability. **3.** Yes, because people do brave things even though they are scared.

Things to do, page 21: 1. Iran 2. Iraq 3. Pakistan 4. China 5. Turkey 6. Egypt 7. Syria 8. India

The Great Alexander the Great Quiz, page 31
1. Achilles **2.** Aristotle **3.** Zeus **4.** He was murdered by one of his bodyguards **5.** Alexandria in Egypt, Kandahar and Herat in Afghanistan **6.** 1896 **7.** Becaphalus **8.** Persia **9.** A Greek soldier **10.** In the city of Persepolis